# VINTAGE RECIPES OF THE 1950S

## A Retro Cookbook that Embodies the Irresistible Flavors of the Past

**Kevin Palmer McDermott**

**© Copyright 2023 by Kevin Palmer McDermott - All rights reserved.**

This document is geared towards providing exact and reliable information in regards to the topic and issue covered. The publication is sold with the idea that the publisher is not required to render accounting, officially permitted, or otherwise, qualified services. If advice is necessary, legal or professional, a practiced individual in the profession should be ordered.

- From a Declaration of Principles which was accepted and approved equally by a Committee of the American Bar Association and a Committee of Publishers and Associations.

In no way is it legal to reproduce, duplicate, or transmit any part of this document in either electronic means or in printed format. Recording of this publication is strictly prohibited and any storage of this document is not allowed unless with written permission from the publisher. All rights reserved.

The information provided herein is stated to be truthful and consistent, in that any liability, in terms of inattention or otherwise, by any usage or abuse of any policies, processes, or directions contained within is the solitary and utter responsibility of the recipient reader. Under no circumstances will any legal responsibility or blame be held against the publisher for any reparation, damages, or monetary loss due to the information herein, either directly or indirectly.

Respective authors own all copyrights not held by the publisher.

The information herein is offered for informational purposes solely, and is universal as so. The presentation of the information is without contract or any type of guarantee assurance.

The trademarks that are used are without any consent, and the publication of the trademark is without permission or backing by the trademark owner. All trademarks and brands within this book are for clarifying purposes only and are the owned by the owners themselves, not affiliated with this document.

# Table of Contents

**Introduction**.................................................................1

**Appetizers & Sides**........................................................3

    Cheese and Olive Skewers....................................3

    Deviled Eggs..............................................................5

    Shrimp Cocktail........................................................7

    Chicken Liver Pate...................................................9

    Crab Dip..................................................................11

    Salami Roll-Ups.....................................................13

    Stuffed Celery with Cream Cheese......................15

    Oysters Rockefeller...............................................17

    Cocktail Meatballs................................................19

    Fried Pickles..........................................................21

    Spinach and Artichoke Dip..................................23

    Crab Rangoon.......................................................25

**Main Dishes**................................................................27

    Meatloaf.................................................................27

    Tuna Casserole......................................................29

    Salisbury Steak.....................................................31

    Beef and Noodles.................................................33

Lemon Chicken..................................................................................................................35

Beef Wellington.................................................................................................................37

Chicken Cordon Bleu........................................................................................................39

Stuffed Peppers.................................................................................................................41

Porcupine Meatballs.........................................................................................................43

Chicken Divan...................................................................................................................45

Beef Bourguignon..............................................................................................................47

Chicken Pot Pie.................................................................................................................49

Beef and Mushroom Pie...................................................................................................51

Chicken Fricassee..............................................................................................................53

**Desserts & Sweets**..............................................................................................................55

Chocolate Caramel Layer Cake......................................................................................55

Cherry Cheesecake...........................................................................................................58

Butterscotch Pudding.......................................................................................................60

Strawberry Shortcake.......................................................................................................62

Coconut Cream Pie...........................................................................................................64

Prune Cake.........................................................................................................................66

Apple Crisp........................................................................................................................68

Pistachio Delight...............................................................................................................70

Orange Chiffon Cake........................................................................................................72

Chocolate Mousse.............................................................................................................74

Rice Pudding.....................................................................................................................76

Molasses Cookies..............................................................................................................78

Peanut Butter Fudge...................................................................................................80

Fruit Cocktail Cake....................................................................................................82

## Drinks...........................................................................................................85

Manhattan................................................................................................................85

Martini.....................................................................................................................87

Negroni....................................................................................................................89

Tom Collins..............................................................................................................91

Gimlet......................................................................................................................93

Singapore Sling........................................................................................................95

Shirley Temple.........................................................................................................97

Roy Rogers..............................................................................................................99

Pink Lemonade......................................................................................................101

Virgin Pina Colada..................................................................................................103

Fruit Punch............................................................................................................105

Root Beer Float......................................................................................................107

Cherry Cola............................................................................................................109

Orange Creamsicle Float........................................................................................111

Chocolate Egg Cream.............................................................................................113

Sparkling Raspberry Limeade.................................................................................115

# Introduction

Welcome to the world of nostalgia and culinary delights! In this book, we will embark on a journey down memory lane to revisit the beloved recipes of the past. This remarkable era is often romanticized for its simplicity and charm, and the kitchen was no exception.

The 1950s brought about a wave of innovation and exploration in the culinary world. As post-war prosperity swept the nation, traditional home cooking underwent a transformation, influenced by exciting developments in the food industry. This cookbook aims to capture the essence of those unforgettable recipes that stood the test of time.

Inside the pages of this book, you will discover a treasure trove of dishes that were staples on dining tables across the country. From retro cocktails and refreshing salads to indulgent desserts and comforting casseroles, these vintage recipes reflect the tastes and trends of a bygone era.

Whether you are a seasoned chef or a novice in the kitchen, this Cookbook offers something for everyone. Revisit the comforting flavors of yesteryear and create new memories with beloved classics. So, grab your apron, sharpen your knives, and let's get started!

# Appetizers & Sides

## Cheese and Olive Skewers

**Preparation Time:** 15 minutes
**Cooking Time:** No cooking required
**Servings:** 4

### Ingredients:

- 16 pitted green or black olives
- 8 ounces of Cheddar cheese, cut into cubes
- 1 small jar of cocktail onions (optional)
- 16 wooden skewers

### Directions:

1. Start by soaking the wooden skewers in water for about 10 minutes. This prevents them from burning while assembling the skewers.
2. Thread one olive onto each skewer, followed by a cube of Cheddar cheese. If desired, you can also add a cocktail onion to each skewer.
3. Repeat the process until each skewer is filled with olives, cheese, and onions if using.
4. Arrange the skewers on a serving platter and refrigerate until ready to serve.

**Nutrition:**
Calories: 130
Fat: 10g
Carbs: 1g
Protein: 8g

# Deviled Eggs

**Preparation Time:** 15 minutes
**Cooking Time:** 10 minutes
**Servings:** 12

### Ingredients:

- 6 eggs
- 2 tablespoons mayonnaise
- 1 teaspoon mustard
- 1/2 teaspoon white vinegar
- 1/4 teaspoon salt
- Paprika, for garnish

### Directions:

1. Place eggs in a saucepan and cover with water. Bring to a boil over medium heat.
2. Once the water boils, remove the saucepan from heat, cover, and let the eggs sit for 10 minutes.
3. Drain the hot water and transfer the eggs to a bowl of ice water. Let them cool for a few minutes.

4. Peel the eggs and slice them in half lengthwise.
5. Gently remove the yolks and place them in a separate bowl. Set the egg white halves aside.
6. Mash the egg yolks with a fork until they are crumbly.
7. Add mayonnaise, mustard, white vinegar, and salt to the mashed yolks. Mix well to combine.
8. Fill each egg white half with the yolk mixture, dividing it evenly among all the halves.
9. Sprinkle deviled eggs with paprika for garnish.
10. Serve immediately or refrigerate until ready to serve.

**Nutrition:**
Calories: 80
Fat: 6g
Carbs: 1g
Protein: 6g

# Shrimp Cocktail

**Preparation Time:** 15 minutes
**Cooking Time:** 5 minutes
**Servings:** 4

### Ingredients:

- 1 pound large shrimp, peeled and deveined
- 1 lemon, cut into wedges
- Ice, for serving
- Cocktail sauce
- Fresh parsley, for garnish

### Directions:

1. Fill a large pot with water and bring it to a boil. Add a pinch of salt to the water.
2. Once the water is boiling, carefully add the shrimp and cook for 2-3 minutes until they turn pink and opaque. Be careful not to overcook them.
3. Use a slotted spoon to transfer the cooked shrimp to a large bowl of ice water. Let them cool completely.
4. Drain the shrimp and pat them dry with paper towels.
5. Arrange a bed of ice in a serving dish or individual cocktail glasses.

6. Place the cooked and cooled shrimp on top of the ice. Squeeze fresh lemon juice over the shrimp.
7. Serve the shrimp cocktail with a side of cocktail sauce for dipping.
8. Garnish with fresh parsley before serving.

**Nutrition:**
Calories: 180
Fat: 2g
Carbs: 5g
Protein: 34g

## Chicken Liver Pate

**Preparation Time:** 20 minutes
**Cooking Time:** 10 minutes
**Servings:** 6

### Ingredients:

- 1 pound chicken livers
- 1/2 cup unsalted butter
- 1 medium onion, finely chopped
- 2 garlic cloves, minced
- 1/4 cup brandy
- 1/4 teaspoon dried thyme
- 1/4 teaspoon dried rosemary
- 1/4 teaspoon ground allspice
- Salt and pepper to taste
- 2 tablespoons heavy cream

### Directions:

1. Rinse and pat dry the chicken livers. Remove any visible fat or connective tissue.

2. In a large skillet, melt the butter over medium heat. Add the chopped onion and minced garlic, and cook until translucent, about 5 minutes.
3. Add the chicken livers to the skillet and cook until they are browned on the outside but still slightly pink on the inside, about 4-5 minutes per side. Do not overcook.
4. Remove the skillet from heat and carefully pour in the brandy. Return the skillet to medium heat and simmer for 2 minutes, allowing the alcohol to burn off.
5. Transfer the contents of the skillet to a food processor. Add the dried thyme, dried rosemary, ground allspice, salt, and pepper. Process until smooth and well combined.
6. With the food processor still running, slowly drizzle in the heavy cream until the mixture reaches a smooth and creamy consistency.
7. Taste and adjust seasonings if necessary.
8. Transfer the pate to a serving dish or ramekins, cover with plastic wrap, and refrigerate for at least 2 hours before serving.
9. Serve chilled with toasted bread or crackers.

**Nutrition:**
Calories: 250
Fat: 20g
Carbs: 3g
Protein: 14g

# Crab Dip

**Preparation Time:** 20 minutes
**Cooking Time:** 25 minutes
**Servings:** 8

## Ingredients:

- 1 lb. fresh crab meat, cooked and shredded
- 8 oz. cream cheese, softened
- 1/2 cup mayonnaise
- 1/4 cup sour cream
- 1/4 cup grated Parmesan cheese
- 1/4 cup chopped green onions
- 2 cloves garlic, minced
- 1 tsp. Worcestershire sauce
- 1 tsp. lemon juice
- 1/2 tsp. Old Bay seasoning
- Salt and pepper to taste

## Directions:

1. Preheat your oven to 350°F (175°C).

2. In a mixing bowl, combine the softened cream cheese, mayonnaise, sour cream, Parmesan cheese, green onions, minced garlic, Worcestershire sauce, lemon juice, Old Bay seasoning, salt, and pepper. Stir until well combined.
3. Gently fold in the shredded crab meat, ensuring it is evenly distributed throughout the mixture.
4. Transfer the crab dip mixture to a greased baking dish or oven-safe serving dish.
5. Bake in the preheated oven for 25 minutes, or until the dip is heated through and bubbly on top.
6. Remove from the oven and let it cool for a few minutes before serving.

**Nutrition:**
Calories: 256
Fat: 21g
Carbs: 3g
Protein: 13g

# Salami Roll-Ups

**Preparation Time:** 10 minutes
**Cooking Time:** None
**Servings:** 12 roll-ups

## Ingredients:

- 12 slices of salami
- 4 ounces of cream cheese, softened
- 2 tablespoons of chopped pickles
- 1 teaspoon of dried dill

## Directions:

1. In a bowl, combine the softened cream cheese, chopped pickles, and dried dill. Mix well until all the ingredients are evenly incorporated.
2. Lay out the salami slices on a flat surface. Spread a thin layer of the cream cheese mixture on each slice.
3. Starting from one end, roll up each slice tightly and secure with a toothpick to hold it together.
4. Arrange the salami roll-ups on a serving platter and refrigerate for at least 30 minutes to allow them to firm up.
5. Serve cold and enjoy!

**Nutrition:**
Calories: 76
Fat: 6g
Carbs: 1g
Protein: 4g

## Stuffed Celery with Cream Cheese

**Preparation Time:** 15 minutes
**Cooking Time:** No cooking required
**Servings:** 4 servings

### Ingredients:

- 8 celery stalks
- 8 oz. cream cheese, softened
- 1/4 cup mayonnaise
- 1/4 cup chopped fresh parsley
- 2 tbsp. chopped green onions
- 1/2 tsp. Worcestershire sauce
- 1/4 tsp. garlic powder
- Salt and pepper to taste

### Directions:

1. Trim the ends of the celery stalks and remove any tough strings. Rinse and pat dry.

2. In a bowl, combine cream cheese, mayonnaise, parsley, green onions, Worcestershire sauce, garlic powder, salt, and pepper. Mix well until smooth and creamy.
3. Fill each celery stalk with the cream cheese mixture, using a spoon or a piping bag for neater results.
4. Arrange the stuffed celery on a serving platter and refrigerate for at least 1 hour before serving.
5. Garnish with additional chopped parsley or green onions if desired.

**Nutrition:**
Calories: 190
Fat: 18g
Carbs: 3g
Protein: 4g

# Oysters Rockefeller

**Preparation Time:** 20 minutes
**Cooking Time:** 10 minutes
**Servings:** 4

## Ingredients:

- 24 fresh oysters
- 1/2 cup unsalted butter, melted
- 1 cup fresh spinach, chopped
- 1/2 cup breadcrumbs
- 1/4 cup grated Parmesan cheese
- 2 tablespoons chopped fresh parsley
- 1 tablespoon chopped fresh tarragon
- 1 tablespoon chopped fresh chives
- 1 clove garlic, minced
- Salt and black pepper to taste
- Lemon wedges, for serving

**Directions:**

1. Preheat your oven to 450°F (230°C).
2. Scrub the oysters under cold water to remove any dirt or debris. Carefully shuck the oysters and place them on a baking sheet.
3. In a skillet over medium heat, melt 1 tablespoon of butter. Add the chopped spinach and cook until wilted, about 2 minutes. Remove from heat and let it cool slightly.
4. In a mixing bowl, combine the breadcrumbs, Parmesan cheese, chopped parsley, tarragon, chives, minced garlic, salt, and black pepper. Mix well.
5. Take a spoonful of the herbed breadcrumb mixture and place it on top of each oyster, pressing it gently to adhere.
6. Drizzle the remaining melted butter over the prepared oysters.
7. Bake in the preheated oven for about 10 minutes, or until the oysters are cooked through and the topping is golden brown.
8. Remove the Oysters Rockefeller from the oven and let them cool for a minute or two.
9. Serve the Oysters Rockefeller hot, with lemon wedges on the side for squeezing over the top.

**Nutrition:**
Calories: 290
Fat: 19g
Carbs: 14g
Protein: 17g

## Cocktail Meatballs

**Preparation Time:** 15 minutes
**Cooking Time:** 30 minutes
**Servings:** 20 meatballs

### Ingredients:

- 1 pound ground beef
- 1/2 cup breadcrumbs
- 1/4 cup milk
- 1/4 cup finely chopped onion
- 1 clove garlic, minced
- 1 large egg
- 1/2 teaspoon salt
- 1/4 teaspoon black pepper
- 1/4 teaspoon paprika

*For the sauce:*

- 1 cup ketchup
- 1/2 cup brown sugar
- 1/4 cup apple cider vinegar
- 1 tablespoon Worcestershire sauce
- 1/2 teaspoon mustard powder

**Directions:**

1. Preheat the oven to 375°F (190°C).
2. In a large bowl, combine the ground beef, breadcrumbs, milk, onion, garlic, egg, salt, black pepper, and paprika. Mix until well combined.
3. Shape the mixture into small meatballs, about 1 inch in diameter, and place them on a baking sheet lined with parchment paper.
4. Bake the meatballs in the preheated oven for 20 minutes, or until cooked through and browned.
5. While the meatballs are baking, prepare the sauce. In a saucepan, combine the ketchup, brown sugar, apple cider vinegar, Worcestershire sauce, and mustard powder. Cook over medium heat, stirring occasionally, until the sauce thickens slightly, about 10 minutes.
6. Once the meatballs are cooked, transfer them to a serving dish and pour the sauce over them. Toss gently to coat the meatballs with the sauce.
7. Serve the cocktail meatballs hot, optionally garnished with chopped parsley, alongside toothpicks for easy serving.

**Nutrition:**
Calories: 120
Fat: 5g
Carbs: 13g
Protein: 6g

# Fried Pickles

**Preparation Time:** 15 minutes
**Cooking Time:** 10 minutes
**Servings:** 4

## Ingredients:

- 1 cup dill pickle slices
- 1 cup all-purpose flour
- 1/2 cup cornmeal
- 1/2 teaspoon paprika
- 1/4 teaspoon cayenne pepper
- 1/2 teaspoon salt
- 1/4 teaspoon black pepper
- 1 cup buttermilk
- Vegetable oil, for frying

## Directions:

1. In a shallow dish, mix together flour, cornmeal, paprika, cayenne pepper, salt, and black pepper.
2. Place the buttermilk in another shallow dish.

3. Dip each pickle slice into the buttermilk, then coat it with the flour mixture, pressing lightly to adhere.
4. Repeat the process for all pickle slices and set them aside on a plate.
5. Heat vegetable oil in a deep skillet or deep-fryer to 375°F (190°C).
6. Carefully add the coated pickle slices to the hot oil in small batches, frying for about 2-3 minutes or until they turn golden brown.
7. Remove the fried pickles using a slotted spoon and place them on a paper towel-lined plate to drain excess oil.
8. Serve the fried pickles hot with your favorite dipping sauce.

**Nutrition:**
Calories: 180
Fat: 5g
Carbs: 30g
Protein: 4g

# Spinach and Artichoke Dip

**Preparation Time:** 15 minutes
**Cooking Time:** 20 minutes
**Servings:** 6

## Ingredients:

- 1 cup frozen spinach, thawed and drained
- 1 can (14 oz.) artichoke hearts, drained and chopped
- 1 cup mayonnaise
- 1 cup sour cream
- 1 cup grated Parmesan cheese
- 1 cup shredded mozzarella cheese
- 2 cloves garlic, minced
- 1/2 teaspoon salt
- 1/4 teaspoon black pepper

## Directions:

1. Preheat the oven to 350°F (175°C).

2. In a mixing bowl, combine the thawed spinach, chopped artichoke hearts, mayonnaise, sour cream, Parmesan cheese, mozzarella cheese, minced garlic, salt, and black pepper. Mix well.
3. Transfer the mixture to a baking dish and spread it evenly.
4. Bake in the preheated oven for 20 minutes, or until the top is golden and bubbly.
5. Remove from the oven and let it cool for a few minutes.
6. Serve the dip warm with your favorite chips, crackers, or bread.

**Nutrition:**
Calories: 345
Fat: 30g
Carbs: 8g
Protein: 12g

# Crab Rangoon

**Preparation Time:** 20 minutes
**Cooking Time:** 10 minutes
**Servings:** 4

## Ingredients:

- 8 oz. crabmeat, drained and flaked
- 4 oz. cream cheese, softened
- 2 green onions, chopped
- 1 clove garlic, minced
- 1/2 teaspoon Worcestershire sauce
- Salt and pepper to taste
- 16 wonton wrappers
- Vegetable oil for frying

## Directions:

1. In a mixing bowl, combine the crabmeat, cream cheese, green onions, garlic, Worcestershire sauce, salt, and pepper. Mix well until all ingredients are evenly incorporated.
2. Place about 1 tablespoon of the crab mixture in the center of each wonton wrapper.

3. Moisten the edges of the wonton wrapper with water and fold them over into a triangle shape. Press firmly to seal.
4. Heat vegetable oil in a deep fryer or a large pot to 350°F (175°C).
5. Carefully place the filled wontons into the hot oil, a few at a time. Fry until golden brown, approximately 2-3 minutes per side.
6. Remove the fried Crab Rangoon using a slotted spoon and transfer them to a paper towel-lined plate to drain off any excess oil.
7. Serve hot with your favorite dipping sauce.

**Nutrition:**
Calories: 254
Fat: 12g
Carbs: 20g
Protein: 16g

# Main Dishes

## Meatloaf

**Preparation Time:** 15 minutes
**Cooking Time:** 1 hour, 15 minutes
**Servings:** 6 servings

### Ingredients:

- 2 lbs. ground beef
- 1 cup breadcrumbs
- 1/2 cup milk
- 1 onion, finely chopped
- 2 cloves garlic, minced
- 2 eggs
- 2 tablespoons Worcestershire sauce
- 1 teaspoon salt
- 1/2 teaspoon black pepper
- 1/4 teaspoon dried thyme
- 1/4 teaspoon dried oregano
- 1/4 teaspoon dried parsley

- 1/4 cup ketchup (for glaze)

**Directions:**

1. Preheat the oven to 350°F (175°C).
2. In a large mixing bowl, combine the ground beef, breadcrumbs, milk, chopped onion, minced garlic, eggs, Worcestershire sauce, salt, black pepper, dried thyme, dried oregano, and dried parsley. Mix well to combine.
3. Shape the meat mixture into a loaf shape and place it in a loaf pan.
4. In a small bowl, mix the ketchup with a tablespoon of Worcestershire sauce. Spread this mixture over the top of the meatloaf.
5. Bake the meatloaf in the preheated oven for 1 hour and 15 minutes, or until the internal temperature reaches 160°F (71°C).
6. Remove the meatloaf from the oven and let it rest for a few minutes before slicing.
7. Serve the meatloaf with your favorite side dishes and enjoy!

**Nutrition:**
Calories: 450
Fat: 25g
Carbs: 15g
Protein: 35g

# Tuna Casserole

**Preparation Time:** 15 minutes
**Cooking Time:** 30 minutes
**Servings:** 4

## Ingredients:

- 6 ounces egg noodles
- 1 can (10.75 ounces) condensed cream of mushroom soup
- 1 cup milk
- 1 cup frozen green peas
- 1 can (6 ounces) tuna, drained and flaked
- 1 cup shredded cheddar cheese
- 1/2 cup crushed potato chips

## Directions:

1. Preheat the oven to 375°F (190°C).
2. Cook the egg noodles according to the package instructions until al dente. Drain and set aside.
3. In a large mixing bowl, combine the condensed cream of mushroom soup and milk. Mix well until smooth.
4. Stir in the frozen green peas and drained tuna into the soup mixture.

5. Add the cooked egg noodles and mix gently until everything is well combined.
6. Transfer the mixture to a greased casserole dish.
7. Sprinkle the shredded cheddar cheese evenly over the top.
8. Sprinkle the crushed potato chips as the final layer.
9. Bake in the preheated oven for about 30 minutes or until the casserole is hot and bubbly, and the cheese is melted and lightly golden.
10. Remove from the oven and let it cool for a few minutes before serving.

**Nutrition:**
Calories: 375
Fat: 19g
Carbs: 25g
Protein: 25g

## Salisbury Steak

**Preparation Time:** 15 minutes
**Cooking Time:** 30 minutes
**Servings:** 4

### Ingredients:

- 1 lb. ground beef
- 1/3 cup breadcrumbs
- 1/4 cup milk
- 1 small onion, finely chopped
- 1 clove garlic, minced
- 1 egg, beaten
- 1/2 tsp. salt
- 1/4 tsp. black pepper
- 1 tbsp. vegetable oil

*For the Onion Gravy:*

- 1 medium onion, thinly sliced
- 2 cups beef broth
- 2 tbsp. all-purpose flour

- 1 tbsp. Worcestershire sauce
- Salt and pepper to taste

**Directions:**

1. In a large bowl, combine ground beef, breadcrumbs, milk, finely chopped onion, minced garlic, beaten egg, salt, and black pepper. Mix well.
2. Shape the mixture into 4 oval-shaped patties.
3. Heat vegetable oil in a skillet over medium heat. Cook the patties for about 4-5 minutes per side until browned. Remove from skillet and set aside.
4. In the same skillet, add the thinly sliced onion for the gravy. Cook until caramelized.
5. Sprinkle flour over the onions and cook for an additional minute, stirring constantly.
6. Gradually pour in beef broth and Worcestershire sauce, stirring constantly to remove any lumps.
7. Bring the mixture to a simmer and cook until the gravy thickens, approximately 5-7 minutes.
8. Return the cooked patties to the skillet, coating them with the onion gravy. Cook for an additional 5 minutes until heated through.
9. Serve the Salisbury steak hot with mashed potatoes, green beans, or your preferred side dish.

**Nutrition:**
Calories: 450
Fat: 28g
Carbs: 20g
Protein: 26g

# Beef and Noodles

**Preparation Time:** 20 minutes
**Cooking Time:** 2 hours
**Servings:** 4

**Ingredients:**

- 1.5 lbs. beef chuck roast, trimmed and cut into small cubes
- 1 onion, finely chopped
- 2 cloves garlic, minced
- 3 carrots, sliced
- 2 stalks celery, sliced
- 4 cups beef broth
- 2 cups water
- 2 bay leaves
- 1 tsp. dried thyme
- 1 tsp. dried parsley
- Salt and black pepper, to taste
- 8 oz. egg noodles

**Directions:**

1. In a large pot or Dutch oven, heat some oil over medium heat. Add the beef cubes and cook until browned on all sides. Remove the beef from the pot and set aside.
2. In the same pot, add the chopped onion and minced garlic. Sauté until the onion becomes translucent.
3. Add the sliced carrots and celery to the pot and cook for a few minutes until they start to soften.
4. Return the beef cubes to the pot. Add the beef broth, water, bay leaves, dried thyme, dried parsley, salt, and black pepper. Give everything a good stir.
5. Bring the mixture to a boil, then reduce the heat to low. Cover the pot and let it simmer for about 1.5 to 2 hours until the beef is tender.
6. In the meantime, cook the egg noodles according to the package instructions. Drain and set aside.
7. Once the beef is tender, remove the bay leaves from the pot. Taste and adjust the seasoning if needed.
8. To serve, divide the cooked egg noodles among bowls and ladle the beef and broth over the noodles. Enjoy!

**Nutrition:**
Calories: 415
Fat: 15g
Carbs: 34g
Protein: 36g

# Lemon Chicken

**Preparation Time:** 15 minutes
**Cooking Time:** 40 minutes
**Servings:** 4

## Ingredients:

- 4 chicken breasts
- 2 lemons
- 1 cup all-purpose flour
- 1 teaspoon salt
- 1 teaspoon pepper
- 1/2 teaspoon paprika
- 1/4 cup butter
- 1/4 cup olive oil
- 1 cup chicken broth
- 1/4 cup fresh lemon juice
- 2 tablespoons chopped fresh parsley

## Directions:

1. In a shallow dish, mix the flour, salt, pepper, and paprika.

2. Dredge the chicken breasts in the flour mixture, shaking off any excess.
3. In a large skillet, melt the butter with the olive oil over medium heat.
4. Add the chicken breasts to the skillet and cook until golden brown on both sides, about 5 minutes per side. Remove the chicken from the skillet and set aside.
5. In the same skillet, add the chicken broth, lemon juice, and zest from one lemon. Bring to a simmer and scrape up any browned bits from the bottom of the skillet.
6. Return the chicken breasts to the skillet and reduce the heat to low. Cover and simmer for 30 minutes or until the chicken is cooked through and tender.
7. Squeeze the juice from the remaining lemon over the chicken and sprinkle with chopped parsley before serving.

**Nutrition:**
Calories: 380
Fat: 17g
Carbs: 12g
Protein: 45g

## Beef Wellington

**Preparation Time**: 30 minutes
**Cooking Time:** 45 minutes
**Servings:** 4

### Ingredients:

- 1 ½ pounds beef fillet
- 2 tablespoons olive oil
- Salt and pepper to taste
- ½ pound mushroom duxelles
- 8 slices of Parma ham
- 500g puff pastry
- 1 egg, beaten (for egg wash)

### Directions:

1. Preheat the oven to 200°C (400°F).
2. Season the beef fillet with salt and pepper.
3. Heat the olive oil in a pan and sear the beef fillet on all sides until browned. Remove from heat and let it cool.
4. Spread the mushroom duxelles evenly over the Parma ham slices.

5. Place the seared beef fillet on top of the mushroom duxelles and wrap it tightly with the ham, sealing it completely.
6. Roll out the puff pastry on a lightly floured surface and wrap the beef and ham parcel with the pastry, sealing it well.
7. Brush the pastry with the beaten egg, ensuring it is fully covered.
8. Place the wrapped beef Wellington on a baking tray and bake in the preheated oven for 30-35 minutes until the pastry is golden brown and the beef is cooked to your desired doneness.
9. Remove from the oven and let it rest for a few minutes before slicing.
10. Serve the Beef Wellington slices with your favorite side dishes.

**Nutrition:**
Calories: 550
Fat: 35g
Carbs: 30g
Protein: 30g

## Chicken Cordon Bleu

**Preparation Time:** 30 minutes
**Cooking Time:** 25 minutes
**Servings:** 4

### Ingredients:

- 4 boneless, skinless chicken breasts
- 4 thin slices of ham
- 4 slices of Swiss cheese
- 1 cup bread crumbs
- 1/2 cup all-purpose flour
- 2 eggs
- Salt and pepper, to taste
- Vegetable oil for frying

### Directions:

1. Preheat the oven to 350°F (175°C).
2. Place each chicken breast between two pieces of plastic wrap and gently pound with a meat mallet until evenly flattened. Season each chicken breast with salt and pepper.

3. Place a slice of ham and a slice of Swiss cheese on top of each flattened chicken breast.
4. Roll up the chicken breasts, securely tucking in the sides to enclose the filling. Use toothpicks to hold the rolls together if needed.
5. In a shallow dish, beat the eggs. In another shallow dish, place the flour, and in a third shallow dish, place the bread crumbs.
6. Dip each chicken roll first in the flour, then in the beaten eggs, and finally coat with bread crumbs.
7. In a large skillet, heat vegetable oil over medium heat. Add the breaded chicken rolls and cook until golden brown on all sides, for about 5 minutes.
8. Transfer the chicken rolls to a baking dish and place in the preheated oven. Bake for 20 minutes or until the chicken is cooked through and the cheese is melted.
9. Remove toothpicks before serving.

**Nutrition:**
Calories: 430
Fat: 22g
Carbs: 16g
Protein: 42g

## Stuffed Peppers

**Preparation Time:** 20 minutes
**Cooking Time:** 1 hour
**Servings:** 4

### Ingredients:

- 4 large bell peppers (any color)
- 1 pound ground beef
- 1/2 cup cooked rice
- 1/2 cup diced onion
- 1/2 cup diced celery
- 1/2 cup diced tomatoes
- 1/4 cup tomato sauce
- 1/4 cup bread crumbs
- 1/4 cup grated Parmesan cheese
- 1 teaspoon Worcestershire sauce
- 1/2 teaspoon salt
- 1/4 teaspoon black pepper

### Directions:

1. Preheat the oven to 350°F (175°C).

2. Cut off the tops of the bell peppers and remove the seeds and membranes.
3. In a large skillet, brown the ground beef over medium heat. Drain any excess fat.
4. Add diced onion and celery to the skillet and cook for 5 minutes until softened.
5. Stir in cooked rice, diced tomatoes, tomato sauce, bread crumbs, Parmesan cheese, Worcestershire sauce, salt, and black pepper. Mix well.
6. Stuff each bell pepper with the beef and rice mixture, filling them evenly.
7. Place the stuffed peppers in a baking dish and cover with foil.
8. Bake for 45 minutes, then remove the foil and bake for an additional 15 minutes to brown the tops.
9. Remove from the oven and let them cool for a few minutes before serving.

**Nutrition:**
Calories: 365
Fat: 15g
Carbs: 26g
Protein: 28g

## Porcupine Meatballs

**Preparation Time:** 15 minutes
**Cooking Time:** 40 minutes
**Servings:** 4

### Ingredients:

- 1 pound ground beef
- 1/2 cup uncooked long-grain rice
- 1/4 cup finely chopped onion
- 1 clove garlic, minced
- 1/4 cup breadcrumbs
- 1/4 cup milk
- 1 egg, beaten
- 1 teaspoon salt
- 1/4 teaspoon black pepper
- 1 (14.5-ounce) can diced tomatoes, un-drained
- 1 (8-ounce) can tomato sauce
- 1 tablespoon Worcestershire sauce
- 1/2 teaspoon dried oregano
- 1/2 teaspoon dried basil

**Directions:**

1. In a large bowl, combine the ground beef, rice, onion, garlic, breadcrumbs, milk, egg, salt, and pepper. Mix well to combine.
2. Shape the mixture into 1 1/2-inch meatballs and place them in a greased baking dish.
3. In a separate bowl, combine the diced tomatoes, tomato sauce, Worcestershire sauce, oregano, and basil. Mix well.
4. Pour the tomato mixture over the meatballs in the baking dish.
5. Cover the dish with foil and bake in a preheated 375°F oven for 30 minutes.
6. Remove the foil and bake for an additional 10 minutes, or until the meatballs are cooked through and the rice is tender.
7. Serve the porcupine meatballs hot, spooning the tomato sauce over them.

**Nutrition:**
Calories: 389
Fat: 20g
Carbs: 23g
Protein: 29g

# Chicken Divan

**Preparation Time:** 20 minutes
**Cooking Time:** 40 minutes
**Servings:** 4

## Ingredients:

- 1 ½ lbs. boneless, skinless chicken breasts
- 1 ½ cups broccoli florets
- 1 can condensed cream of chicken soup
- ½ cup mayonnaise
- ½ cup sour cream
- 1 teaspoon lemon juice
- 1 teaspoon curry powder (optional)
- Salt and pepper, to taste
- Cooking spray
- 1 cup shredded cheddar cheese

**Directions:**

1. Preheat your oven to 350°F (175°C). Grease a 9x13-inch baking dish with cooking spray.
2. In a large pot, bring water to a boil. Add the chicken breasts and cook for about 15 minutes until fully cooked. Remove the chicken from the pot and set aside to cool.
3. In the same pot, blanch the broccoli florets in boiling water for 2-3 minutes until slightly tender. Drain and set aside.
4. In a medium bowl, combine the condensed cream of chicken soup, mayonnaise, sour cream, lemon juice, curry powder (if desired), salt, and pepper. Mix well.
5. Cut the cooled chicken breasts into bite-sized pieces and place them in the greased baking dish. Arrange the blanched broccoli evenly over the chicken.
6. Pour the sauce mixture over the chicken and broccoli, ensuring everything is well-coated.
7. Sprinkle shredded cheddar cheese evenly on top of the casserole.
8. Bake in the preheated oven for 30-35 minutes or until the chicken is heated through and the cheese is melted and bubbly.
9. Remove from the oven and let it cool for a few minutes before serving.

**Nutrition:**
Calories: 380
Fat: 25g
Carbs: 9g
Protein: 30g

# Beef Bourguignon

**Preparation Time:** 30 minutes
**Cooking Time:** 2 hours, 30 minutes
**Servings:** 4

## Ingredients:

- 1.5 lbs. beef chuck, cut into 1-inch cubes
- 4 slices bacon, chopped
- 1 onion, diced
- 2 carrots, sliced
- 2 cloves garlic, minced
- 1 cup red wine (such as Burgundy or Pinot Noir)
- 2 cups beef broth
- 2 tablespoons tomato paste
- 1 bay leaf
- 1 sprig thyme
- 1 pound small white mushrooms
- 2 tablespoons butter
- Salt and black pepper to taste
- Chopped fresh parsley for garnish

**Directions:**

1. In a large Dutch oven or heavy-bottomed pot, cook the chopped bacon over medium heat until crispy. Remove the bacon and set aside, leaving the drippings in the pot.
2. Sear the beef cubes in the bacon drippings until browned on all sides. Remove the beef and set aside.
3. In the same pot, add the diced onion, sliced carrots, and minced garlic. Cook until the vegetables are softened.
4. Return the cooked bacon and seared beef to the pot. Pour in the red wine and beef broth. Stir in the tomato paste, bay leaf, and thyme. Season with salt and black pepper.
5. Bring the mixture to a simmer, then reduce the heat to low. Cover and let it cook for 2 hours, or until the beef is tender.
6. While the beef is simmering, melt the butter in a separate skillet. Add the mushrooms and sauté until they are golden and tender.
7. Add the sautéed mushrooms to the beef stew and let it simmer for another 30 minutes to allow the flavors to blend.
8. Discard the bay leaf and thyme sprig before serving. Garnish with chopped fresh parsley.
9. Serve the Beef Bourguignon hot with crusty bread or mashed potatoes.

**Nutrition:**
Calories: 450
Fat: 20g
Carbs: 10g
Protein: 50g

## Chicken Pot Pie

**Preparation Time:** 20 minutes
**Cooking Time:** 30 minutes
**Servings:** 6-8 servings

### Ingredients:

- 2 cups cooked chicken, diced
- 1 cup frozen mixed vegetables (peas, carrots, corn)
- 1 small onion, diced
- 2 cloves garlic, minced
- 1/4 cup butter
- 1/4 cup all-purpose flour
- 2 cups chicken broth
- 1/2 cup milk
- 1 teaspoon salt
- 1/2 teaspoon black pepper
- 1/2 teaspoon dried thyme
- 2 prepared pie crusts

### Directions:

1. Preheat the oven to 400°F (200°C).

2. In a large skillet, melt the butter over medium heat. Add the diced onion and minced garlic, and sauté until the onion becomes translucent.
3. Add the all-purpose flour to the skillet and stir well, cooking for about 1 minute to create a roux.
4. Gradually pour in the chicken broth and milk, while stirring constantly. Continue cooking and stirring until the mixture thickens.
5. Add the cooked chicken, frozen mixed vegetables, salt, black pepper, and dried thyme to the skillet. Stir well to combine all the ingredients. Cook for a few more minutes until the vegetables are slightly tender.
6. Remove the skillet from heat and let the filling mixture cool slightly.
7. Roll out one prepared pie crust and line a greased 9-inch (23 cm) pie plate with it.
8. Pour the cooled filling mixture into the pie crust-lined plate.
9. Roll out the second pie crust and place it on top of the filling. Seal the edges and press down with a fork to create a decorative border.
10. Cut slits on the top crust to allow steam to escape while baking.
11. Place the pot pie in the preheated oven and bake for about 30 minutes or until the crust turns golden brown and the filling is bubbly.
12. Remove from the oven and let it cool for a few minutes before serving.

**Nutrition:**
Calories: 320
Fat: 18g
Carbs: 26g
Protein: 14g

# Beef and Mushroom Pie

**Preparation Time:** 20 minutes
**Cooking Time:** 1 hour and 30 minutes
**Servings:** 6

## Ingredients:

- 1 ½ pounds beef stew meat, cut into chunks
- 8 ounces mushrooms, sliced
- 1 onion, chopped
- 2 cloves garlic, minced
- 2 tablespoons vegetable oil
- 2 tablespoons all-purpose flour
- 1 cup beef broth
- 1 cup red wine
- 1 teaspoon Worcestershire sauce
- 1 teaspoon dried thyme
- Salt and pepper, to taste
- 1 package refrigerated pie crusts

**Directions:**

1. Preheat the oven to 375°F (190°C).
2. In a large skillet, heat the vegetable oil over medium heat. Add the beef stew meat, season with salt and pepper, and cook until browned on all sides. Remove the beef from the skillet and set aside.
3. In the same skillet, add the onions and garlic. Cook until the onions are translucent.
4. Add the sliced mushrooms to the skillet and cook until they release their moisture and start to brown.
5. Sprinkle the flour over the mushrooms and onions, and stir to coat.
6. Gradually add the beef broth and red wine, stirring constantly to avoid any lumps.
7. Add the Worcestershire sauce and dried thyme. Season with salt and pepper to taste.
8. Return the beef stew meat to the skillet and stir to combine with the sauce.
9. Cover the skillet and simmer for 1 hour, or until the beef is tender.
10. While the meat is simmering, roll out one pie crust and place it in a pie dish.
11. Pour the beef and mushroom mixture into the pie dish.
12. Roll out the second pie crust and cover the filling. Seal the edges and cut slits in the top crust to allow steam to escape.
13. Place the pie on a baking sheet and bake for 30-35 minutes, or until the crust is golden brown.
14. Remove from the oven and let it cool for a few minutes before serving.

**Nutrition:**
Calories: 400
Fat: 20g
Carbs: 30g
Protein: 25g

# Chicken Fricassee

**Preparation Time:** 20 minutes
**Cooking Time:** 1 hour
**Servings:** 4

## Ingredients:

- 1 whole chicken, cut into pieces
- 1/4 cup all-purpose flour
- 2 tablespoons butter
- 1 onion, chopped
- 2 cloves of garlic, minced
- 1 cup chicken broth
- 1 cup milk
- 1/2 cup heavy cream
- 1 teaspoon dried thyme
- Salt and pepper to taste
- Fresh parsley for garnish

**Directions:**

1. In a shallow dish, season the flour with salt and pepper. Dredge the chicken pieces in the flour, shaking off any excess.
2. In a large skillet, melt the butter over medium-high heat. Add the chicken pieces and cook until golden brown on all sides. Remove the chicken from the skillet and set aside.
3. In the same skillet, add the chopped onion and minced garlic. Sauté until the onion is translucent and fragrant.
4. Add the chicken broth to the skillet and scrape any browned bits from the bottom. Bring it to a simmer.
5. Return the chicken pieces to the skillet and add the dried thyme. Cover and cook over low heat for about 45 minutes, or until the chicken is cooked through and tender.
6. Remove the chicken pieces from the skillet and keep them warm.
7. In a separate bowl, whisk together the milk and heavy cream. Slowly pour this mixture into the skillet, stirring constantly.
8. Simmer the sauce for a few minutes until it thickens. Season with salt and pepper to taste.
9. Return the chicken pieces to the skillet and simmer for an additional 5 minutes to allow the flavors to meld together.
10. Remove from heat and garnish with fresh parsley before serving.

**Nutrition:**
Calories: 400
Fat: 25g
Carbs: 10g
Protein: 35g

# Desserts & Sweets

## Chocolate Caramel Layer Cake

**Preparation Time:** 30 minutes
**Cooking Time:** 45 minutes
**Servings:** 12

### Ingredients:

- 1 and 3/4 cups all-purpose flour
- 3/4 cup unsweetened cocoa powder
- 1 and 1/2 teaspoons baking powder
- 1 and 1/2 teaspoons baking soda
- 1 teaspoon salt
- 2 cups granulated sugar
- 3 large eggs
- 1 cup buttermilk
- 1/2 cup vegetable oil
- 2 teaspoons vanilla extract
- 1 cup hot water

*Caramel Sauce:*

- 1 cup granulated sugar
- 1/4 cup water
- 1/2 cup heavy cream
- 2 tablespoons unsalted butter
- 1/2 teaspoon salt
- 1 teaspoon vanilla extract

*Caramel Frosting:*

- 1 cup unsalted butter, softened
- 2 cups powdered sugar
- 1/4 cup caramel sauce (from the recipe above)
- 1/2 teaspoon vanilla extract
- 1/4 teaspoon salt

**Directions:**

1. Preheat the oven to 350°F (175°C). Grease and flour three 9-inch round cake pans.
2. In a large mixing bowl, sift together the flour, cocoa powder, baking powder, baking soda, and salt. Set aside.
3. In a separate bowl, beat together the sugar, eggs, buttermilk, vegetable oil, and vanilla extract until well combined.
4. Gradually add the wet ingredients to the dry ingredients, mixing until just combined.
5. Stir in the hot water, mixing until the batter is smooth and well incorporated.
6. Divide the batter equally among the prepared cake pans. Smooth the tops with a spatula.

7. Bake for approximately 25-30 minutes, or until a toothpick inserted into the center of the cakes comes out clean.
8. While the cakes are baking, prepare the caramel sauce. In a medium saucepan, combine the granulated sugar and water over medium heat. Stir until the sugar has dissolved.
9. Allow the mixture to come to a boil without stirring, until it turns a deep amber color. Remove from heat and carefully whisk in the heavy cream, butter, salt, and vanilla extract until smooth. Set aside to cool.
10. Once the cakes are done, remove them from the oven and let them cool in the pans for 10 minutes. Then transfer them to a wire rack to cool completely.
11. To make the caramel frosting, beat the softened butter in a mixing bowl until creamy. Gradually add the powdered sugar and beat until light and fluffy.
12. Mix in 1/4 cup of the caramel sauce, vanilla extract, and salt until well combined.
13. Place one cake layer on a serving plate or cake stand. Spread a layer of caramel frosting on top. Drizzle with some caramel sauce.
14. Repeat this process with the second cake layer. Finally, place the third cake layer on top and frost the entire cake with the remaining caramel frosting.
15. Drizzle extra caramel sauce over the top of the cake for decoration.

**Nutrition:**
Calories: 450
Fat: 22g
Carbs: 63g
Protein: 4g

## Cherry Cheesecake

**Preparation Time:** 20 minutes
**Cooking Time:** 1 hour
**Servings:** 8

### Ingredients:

- 1 ½ cups graham cracker crumbs
- 1/3 cup melted butter
- 3 packages (8 oz. each) cream cheese, softened
- 1 cup sugar
- 1 teaspoon vanilla extract
- 3 eggs
- 1 can (21 oz.) cherry pie filling

### Directions:

1. Preheat the oven to 325°F (162°C).
2. In a mixing bowl, combine the graham cracker crumbs and melted butter. Press the mixture evenly onto the bottom of a 9-inch springform pan to form the crust.
3. In a large mixing bowl, beat the cream cheese until smooth. Add the sugar and vanilla extract, and continue to beat until well combined.

4. Beat in the eggs, one at a time, ensuring each egg is fully incorporated before adding the next.
5. Pour the cream cheese mixture into the prepared crust, spreading it evenly.
6. Bake in the preheated oven for about 55-60 minutes, or until the center is set and the top is lightly browned.
7. Remove the cheesecake from the oven and let it cool in the pan on a wire rack for about 1 hour.
8. Once cooled, refrigerate the cheesecake for at least 4 hours, or overnight if possible.
9. Before serving, carefully remove the sides of the springform pan.
10. Top the cheesecake with the cherry pie filling, spreading it evenly over the surface.

**Nutrition:**
Calories: 395
Fat: 24g
Carbs: 40g
Protein: 6g

# Butterscotch Pudding

**Preparation Time:** 15 minutes
**Cooking Time:** 15 minutes
**Servings:** 4

## Ingredients:

- 1/2 cup packed brown sugar
- 2 tablespoons cornstarch
- 1/4 teaspoon salt
- 2 3/4 cups whole milk
- 3 large egg yolks
- 2 tablespoons unsalted butter
- 1 teaspoon vanilla extract

## Directions:

1. In a medium saucepan, combine the brown sugar, cornstarch, and salt. Gradually whisk in the milk until smooth.
2. Place the saucepan over medium heat and cook, stirring constantly, until the mixture thickens and comes to a simmer.

3. In a separate bowl, lightly beat the egg yolks. Gradually whisk in about 1/2 cup of the hot milk mixture to temper the yolks.
4. Slowly pour the tempered yolks back into the saucepan, whisking constantly. Cook for an additional 2 minutes, stirring continuously.
5. Remove the saucepan from heat and stir in the butter and vanilla extract until fully incorporated.
6. Pour the pudding into individual serving dishes or a large bowl. Cover with plastic wrap, pressing it directly onto the surface of the pudding to prevent a skin from forming.
7. Refrigerate for at least 2 hours, or until set.

**Nutrition:**
Calories: 250
Fat: 9g
Carbs: 38g
Protein: 6g

# Strawberry Shortcake

**Preparation Time:** 15 minutes
**Cooking Time:** 15 minutes
**Servings:** 6

## Ingredients:

- 2 cups all-purpose flour
- 2 tablespoons granulated sugar
- 1 tablespoon baking powder
- 1/2 teaspoon salt
- 1/2 cup cold unsalted butter, cubed
- 3/4 cup milk
- 2 pints fresh strawberries, hulled and sliced
- 1/4 cup granulated sugar
- Whipped cream, for serving

## Directions:

1. Preheat the oven to 425°F (220°C). Line a baking sheet with parchment paper.
2. In a large bowl, whisk together the flour, sugar, baking powder, and salt.

3. Add the cold butter to the flour mixture. Using a pastry cutter or your fingers, cut the butter into the flour until the mixture resembles coarse crumbs.
4. Gradually add the milk, mixing until the dough comes together.
5. Turn the dough out onto a lightly floured surface and knead it a few times until it forms a smooth ball.
6. Roll out the dough to a thickness of about 1/2 inch. Using a biscuit cutter, cut out rounds of dough and place them onto the prepared baking sheet.
7. Bake for 12-15 minutes, or until the biscuits are golden brown. Allow them to cool slightly on a wire rack.
8. In the meantime, combine the sliced strawberries and sugar in a bowl. Let the strawberries macerate for about 10 minutes, until they release their juices.
9. To assemble the strawberry shortcakes, split the biscuits in half horizontally. Spoon a generous amount of strawberries on the bottom half of each biscuit. Top with a dollop of whipped cream and then place the other half of the biscuit on top.
10. Serve immediately and enjoy!

**Nutrition:**
Calories: 312
Fat: 15g
Carbs: 40g
Protein: 5g

# Coconut Cream Pie

**Preparation Time:** 30 minutes
**Cooking Time:** 15 minutes
**Servings:** 8

## Ingredients:

- 1 9-inch pre-baked pie crust
- 2/3 cup granulated sugar
- 1/4 cup cornstarch
- 1/4 teaspoon salt
- 3 cups whole milk
- 4 large egg yolks, lightly beaten
- 2 tablespoons unsalted butter
- 1 teaspoon vanilla extract
- 1 cup sweetened shredded coconut
- 1 cup heavy cream
- 2 tablespoons powdered sugar
- 1/2 teaspoon vanilla extract
- 1/4 cup toasted coconut flakes (optional)

**Directions:**

1. In a medium saucepan, combine the granulated sugar, cornstarch, and salt. Gradually whisk in the milk until smooth.
2. Place the saucepan over medium heat and cook, stirring constantly, until the mixture thickens and comes to a boil. Boil for 1 minute, then remove from heat.
3. In a separate bowl, whisk the egg yolks. Gradually whisk about 1 cup of the hot milk mixture into the egg yolks to temper them. Pour the tempered egg mixture back into the saucepan with the remaining milk mixture.
4. Place the saucepan back over medium heat and cook, stirring constantly, until the mixture thickens and comes to a boil. Boil for 1 minute, then remove from heat.
5. Stir in the butter, vanilla extract, and 3/4 cup of shredded coconut until well combined. Let the mixture cool for about 15 minutes.
6. Pour the coconut filling into the pre-baked pie crust and smooth the top with a spatula. Place a piece of plastic wrap directly on the surface of the filling to prevent a skin from forming. Refrigerate for at least 4 hours or until set.
7. In a chilled mixing bowl, whip the heavy cream, powdered sugar, and vanilla extract until soft peaks form.
8. Remove the plastic wrap from the pie filling and spread the whipped cream over the top. Sprinkle with the remaining 1/4 cup of shredded coconut and toasted coconut flakes, if desired.
9. Serve chilled and enjoy!

**Nutrition:**
Calories: 420
Fat: 26g
Carbs: 43g
Protein: 7g

# Prune Cake

**Preparation Time:** 15 minutes
**Cooking Time:** 45 minutes
**Servings:** 12

**Ingredients:**

- 1 cup pitted prunes, chopped
- 1 cup boiling water
- 2 cups all-purpose flour
- 1 teaspoon baking powder
- 1 teaspoon baking soda
- ½ teaspoon salt
- 1 teaspoon cinnamon
- ½ teaspoon nutmeg
- ½ teaspoon allspice
- ½ cup unsalted butter, softened
- 1 cup granulated sugar
- 2 large eggs
- 1 teaspoon vanilla extract

**Directions:**

1. Preheat the oven to 350°F (175°C). Grease and flour a 9-inch square baking pan.
2. In a small bowl, pour boiling water over the chopped prunes. Let them soak for 10 minutes, then drain well.
3. In a medium bowl, whisk together the flour, baking powder, baking soda, salt, cinnamon, nutmeg, and allspice. Set aside.
4. In a large mixing bowl, cream together the butter and sugar until light and fluffy.
5. Beat in the eggs, one at a time, followed by the vanilla extract.
6. Gradually add the dry ingredients to the butter mixture, alternating with the drained prunes. Begin and end with the dry ingredients, mixing until just combined.
7. Pour the batter into the prepared baking pan and smooth the top with a spatula.
8. Bake for 40-45 minutes, or until a toothpick inserted into the center comes out clean.
9. Let the cake cool in the pan for 10 minutes, then transfer it to a wire rack to cool completely.
10. Once cooled, optionally dust the cake with powdered sugar or frost with cream cheese frosting before serving.

**Nutrition:**
Calories: 245
Fat: 8g
Carbs: 42g
Protein: 3g

# Apple Crisp

**Preparation Time:** 15 minutes
**Cooking Time:** 40 minutes
**Servings:** 6

### Ingredients:

- 6 cups peeled, cored, and sliced apples
- 1 cup all-purpose flour
- 1 cup rolled oats
- 1 cup packed brown sugar
- 1/2 cup unsalted butter, melted
- 1 teaspoon ground cinnamon
- 1/2 teaspoon ground nutmeg
- 1/4 teaspoon salt

### Directions:

1. Preheat your oven to 375°F (190°C).
2. In a large mixing bowl, combine the sliced apples with 1/4 cup of brown sugar, cinnamon, nutmeg, and salt. Toss until the apples are well coated.
3. In a separate bowl, mix together the flour, rolled oats, remaining 3/4 cup of brown sugar, and melted butter until crumbly.

4. Take half of the oat mixture and press it into the bottom of a lightly greased 9x9-inch baking dish.
5. Spread the apple mixture evenly over the oat mixture.
6. Sprinkle the remaining oat mixture on top of the apples, covering them evenly.
7. Bake in the preheated oven for about 40 minutes or until the top is golden brown and the apples are tender.
8. Remove from the oven and let it cool for a few minutes before serving.

**Nutrition:**
Calories: 320
Fat: 12g
Carbs: 53g
Protein: 3g

# Pistachio Delight

**Preparation Time:** 15 minutes
**Cooking Time:** 10 minutes
**Servings:** 8

## Ingredients:

- 2 cups graham cracker crumbs
- 1/2 cup melted butter
- 1 cup chopped pistachios
- 1 cup + 2 tablespoons granulated sugar, divided
- 2 packages (3.4 oz. each) instant pistachio pudding mix
- 3 cups cold milk
- 1 cup heavy cream
- 1/2 teaspoon vanilla extract
- Whipped cream and additional pistachios for garnish (optional)

## Directions:

1. In a mixing bowl, combine graham cracker crumbs, melted butter, 2 tablespoons of sugar, and chopped pistachios. Mix until well combined.

2. Press the mixture into the bottom of a 9x13-inch baking dish to form the crust. Set aside.
3. In a separate bowl, whisk together the instant pistachio pudding mix, cold milk, and 1 cup of sugar for about 2 minutes until it thickens.
4. Pour the pudding mixture over the graham cracker crust, spreading evenly.
5. In another bowl, whip the heavy cream and vanilla extract until stiff peaks form.
6. Spread the whipped cream over the pudding layer, creating a smooth top.
7. Refrigerate for at least 4 hours or until set.
8. Before serving, garnish with whipped cream and additional chopped pistachios if desired.
9. Enjoy your delicious 1950s Pistachio Delight!

**Nutrition:**
Calories: 342
Fat: 17g
Carbs: 42g
Protein: 5g

# Orange Chiffon Cake

**Preparation Time:** 25 minutes
**Cooking Time:** 45 minutes
**Servings:** 8-10 servings

### Ingredients:

- 2 cups cake flour
- 1 1/2 cups granulated sugar
- 1 tablespoon baking powder
- 1/2 teaspoon salt
- 1/2 cup vegetable oil
- 5 large eggs, separated
- 3/4 cup fresh orange juice
- 1 tablespoon orange zest
- 1/2 teaspoon cream of tartar

### Directions:

1. Preheat the oven to 325°F (165°C) and prepare a 10-inch tube pan by greasing the bottom and sides lightly.

2. In a large mixing bowl, combine the cake flour, sugar, baking powder, and salt. Whisk together to ensure they are well mixed.
3. Make a well in the center of the dry ingredients and add the vegetable oil, egg yolks, orange juice, and orange zest. Mix until smooth and well combined.
4. In a separate mixing bowl, beat the egg whites and cream of tartar until stiff peaks form.
5. Gently fold the beaten egg whites into the batter, making sure not to overmix.
6. Pour the batter into the prepared tube pan and smooth the top with a spatula.
7. Bake in the preheated oven for about 45 minutes, or until a toothpick inserted into the center comes out clean.
8. Once done, remove the cake from the oven and run a knife around the edges to loosen it from the pan. Let it cool upside down on a wire rack for about an hour.
9. Once completely cooled, run a knife again around the edges to release the cake from the pan. Invert onto a serving plate.

**Nutrition:**
Calories: 320
Fat: 12g
Carbs: 48g
Protein: 6g

# Chocolate Mousse

**Preparation Time:** 15 minutes
**Cooking Time:** 10 minutes
**Servings:** 4

## Ingredients:

- ½ pound dark chocolate
- 4 eggs, separated
- 1/4 cup granulated sugar
- 1/4 teaspoon salt
- 1 teaspoon vanilla extract
- 1 cup heavy cream

## Directions:

1. In a heatproof bowl, melt the dark chocolate over a saucepan of simmering water. Stir until smooth and then remove from heat. Let it cool slightly.
2. In a separate bowl, beat the egg yolks with the sugar, salt, and vanilla extract until creamy and pale yellow.
3. Gradually pour the melted chocolate into the egg yolk mixture, whisking continuously until well combined.

4. In a chilled bowl, whip the heavy cream until soft peaks form. Set aside.
5. In another clean bowl, beat the egg whites until stiff peaks form.
6. Gently fold the whipped cream into the chocolate mixture until fully incorporated.
7. Then, fold in the beaten egg whites, being careful not to overmix.
8. Spoon the chocolate mousse into serving glasses or bowls.
9. Refrigerate for at least 2 hours, or until set.
10. Serve chilled and garnish with grated chocolate or whipped cream if desired.

**Nutrition:**
Calories: 360
Fat: 28g
Carbs: 26g
Protein: 7g

# Rice Pudding

**Preparation Time:** 15 minutes
**Cooking Time:** 1 hour
**Servings:** 6

### Ingredients:

- 1 cup white rice
- 2 cups milk
- 1/2 cup sugar
- 1/4 teaspoon salt
- 1 teaspoon vanilla extract
- 1/2 teaspoon ground cinnamon
- 2 eggs, beaten
- Optional: raisins for garnish

### Directions:

1. In a medium saucepan, combine the rice, milk, sugar, and salt. Cook over medium heat, stirring occasionally, until the mixture comes to a gentle boil.

2. Reduce the heat to low and simmer for about 45 minutes, or until the rice is cooked and the mixture thickens. Stir occasionally to prevent the rice from sticking to the bottom of the pan.
3. In a small bowl, whisk together the beaten eggs, vanilla extract, and ground cinnamon.
4. Slowly pour the egg mixture into the rice mixture, stirring continuously. Cook for an additional 5 minutes, or until the pudding thickens further.
5. Remove from heat and let cool for a few minutes.
6. Serve the rice pudding warm or chilled. If desired, garnish with raisins for added flavor and texture.

**Nutrition:**
Calories: 230
Fat: 2g
Carbs: 45g
Protein: 6g

# Molasses Cookies

**Preparation Time:** 15 minutes
**Cooking Time:** 10-12 minutes
**Servings:** 24 cookies

## Ingredients:

- 1/2 cup unsalted butter, softened
- 1 cup granulated sugar
- 1/4 cup molasses
- 1 egg
- 2 cups all-purpose flour
- 2 teaspoons baking soda
- 1/2 teaspoon salt
- 1 teaspoon ground cinnamon
- 1/2 teaspoon ground ginger
- 1/4 teaspoon ground cloves
- Additional granulated sugar for rolling

**Directions:**

1. Preheat your oven to 375°F (190°C) and line a baking sheet with parchment paper.
2. In a large mixing bowl, cream together the butter and granulated sugar until light and fluffy.
3. Add the molasses and egg, and mix until well combined.
4. In a separate bowl, whisk together the flour, baking soda, salt, cinnamon, ginger, and cloves.
5. Gradually add the dry ingredients to the wet ingredients, mixing until just combined.
6. Roll the dough into 24 equal-sized balls.
7. Roll each ball in granulated sugar to coat.
8. Place the coated dough balls onto the prepared baking sheet, spacing them about 2 inches apart.
9. Bake in the preheated oven for 10-12 minutes, or until the edges are set and the centers are slightly soft.
10. Remove from the oven and allow the cookies to cool on the baking sheet for 5 minutes before transferring them to a wire rack to cool completely.

**Nutrition:**
Calories: 139
Fat: 5g
Carbs: 22g
Protein: 1g

# Peanut Butter Fudge

**Preparation Time:** 10 minutes
**Cooking Time:** 15 minutes
**Servings:** 36 pieces

## Ingredients:

- 2 cups granulated sugar
- 1/2 cup milk
- 1 tsp. pure vanilla extract
- 3/4 cup creamy peanut butter
- 1 cup marshmallow creme

## Directions:

1. In a large saucepan, combine sugar and milk over medium heat. Stir until the sugar dissolves completely.
2. Bring the mixture to a boil. Once boiling, reduce the heat to low and simmer for 5 minutes, stirring occasionally.
3. Remove the saucepan from heat and add vanilla extract, peanut butter, and marshmallow creme. Stir well until all the ingredients are fully incorporated and smooth.

4. Pour the fudge mixture into a greased 8x8 inch square pan. Spread the mixture evenly using a spatula.
5. Let the fudge cool at room temperature until it hardens, typically around 2 hours.
6. Once cooled and set, cut the fudge into 36 pieces.

**Nutrition:**
Calories: 85
Fat: 3.8g
Carbs: 11.9g
Protein: 1.4g

# Fruit Cocktail Cake

**Preparation Time:** 15 minutes
**Cooking Time:** 45 minutes
**Servings:** 12

## Ingredients:

- 1 can (15 ounces) fruit cocktail, un-drained
- 2 cups all-purpose flour
- 1 1/2 cups granulated sugar
- 2 teaspoons baking soda
- 1/2 teaspoon salt
- 2 eggs
- 1 teaspoon vanilla extract
- 1/2 cup chopped walnuts (optional)

*For the frosting:*

- 1/2 cup unsalted butter, softened
- 2 cups powdered sugar
- 1 teaspoon vanilla extract
- 2-3 tablespoons milk

**Directions:**

1. Preheat the oven to 350°F (175°C). Grease and flour a 9x13-inch baking pan.
2. In a large mixing bowl, combine the fruit cocktail (with the syrup), flour, sugar, baking soda, salt, eggs, and vanilla extract. Stir until well combined.
3. If desired, fold in the chopped walnuts.
4. Pour the batter into the prepared baking pan and spread it evenly.
5. Bake for 45 minutes or until a toothpick inserted into the center comes out clean.
6. Remove the cake from the oven and let it cool completely in the pan on a wire rack.

*For the frosting:*

7. In a mixing bowl, beat the softened butter until creamy.
8. Gradually add powdered sugar and vanilla extract, beating well after each addition.
9. Add milk, one tablespoon at a time, until the desired consistency is achieved.
10. Spread the frosting evenly over the cooled cake.
11. Cut into squares and serve.

**Nutrition:**
Calories: 297
Fat: 10g
Carbs: 50g
Protein: 3g

# Drinks

## Manhattan

**Preparation Time:** 5 minutes
**Cooking Time:** None
**Servings:** 1

### Ingredients:

- 2 ounces whiskey (preferably bourbon)
- 1 ounce sweet vermouth
- 2 dashes Angostura bitters
- Maraschino cherry, for garnish (optional)
- Orange peel, for garnish (optional)
- Ice cubes

### Directions:

1. Fill a mixing glass or shaker with ice cubes.
2. Pour in the whiskey, sweet vermouth, and Angostura bitters.

3. Stir well using a bar spoon for about 30 seconds, ensuring all the ingredients are thoroughly combined and chilled.
4. Strain the mixture into a chilled cocktail glass.
5. Garnish with a maraschino cherry or twist of orange peel, if desired.
6. Serve and enjoy the classic 1950s Manhattan cocktail!

**Nutrition:**
Calories: 180
Fat: 0g
Carbs: 7g
Protein: 0g

## Martini

**Preparation Time:** 5 minutes
**Cooking Time:** None
**Servings:** 1

### Ingredients:

- 2 1/2 ounces gin
- 1/2 ounce dry vermouth
- 1-2 dashes orange bitters (optional)
- Lemon twist or olive, for garnish

### Directions:

1. Fill a mixing glass or shaker with ice cubes.
2. Add gin, dry vermouth, and orange bitters (if using).
3. Stir gently for about 30 seconds to chill the drink.
4. Strain the mixture into a chilled martini glass.
5. Garnish with a lemon twist or olive.

**Nutrition:**
Calories: 195
Fat: 0g
Carbs: 1g
Protein: 0g

# Negroni

**Preparation Time:** 5 minutes
**Cooking Time:** None
**Servings:** 1

## Ingredients:

- 1 oz. Campari
- 1 oz. gin
- 1 oz. sweet vermouth
- Orange twist, for garnish

## Directions:

1. Fill a mixing glass or shaker with ice.
2. Pour in Campari, gin, and sweet vermouth.
3. Stir gently for about 30 seconds.
4. Strain the mixture into an old-fashioned glass filled with ice.
5. Garnish with an orange twist.
6. Serve and enjoy!

**Nutrition:**
Calories: 205
Fat: 0g
Carbs: 11g
Protein: 0g

# Tom Collins

**Preparation Time:** 5 minutes
**Cooking Time:** None
**Servings:** 1

## Ingredients:

- 2 oz. gin
- 1 oz. lemon juice
- 1/2 oz. simple syrup
- Club soda
- Ice cubes
- Lemon slice and cherry (for garnish)

## Directions:

1. Fill a Collins glass with ice cubes.
2. Pour gin, lemon juice, and simple syrup into the glass.
3. Stir gently to combine the ingredients.
4. Top up the glass with club soda.
5. Garnish with a lemon slice and cherry.
6. Serve and enjoy!

**Nutrition:**
Calories: 180
Fat: 0g
Carbs: 8g
Protein: 0g

# Gimlet

**Preparation Time:** 5 minutes
**Cooking Time:** None
**Servings:** 1

## Ingredients:

- 2 ounces gin
- 1 ounce lime juice (freshly squeezed)
- 1/2 ounce simple syrup
- Lime wedge or wheel, for garnish

## Directions:

1. Fill a cocktail shaker with ice cubes.
2. Add gin, lime juice, and simple syrup to the shaker.
3. Shake vigorously for about 15 seconds to chill the ingredients.
4. Strain the mixture into a chilled cocktail glass.
5. Garnish with a lime wedge or wheel.
6. Serve and enjoy!

**Nutrition:**
Calories: 160
Fat: 0g
Carbs: 8g
Protein: 0g

# Singapore Sling

**Preparation Time:** 5 minutes
**Cooking Time:** None
**Servings:** 1

## Ingredients:

- 1.5 oz. gin
- 1 oz. pineapple juice
- 0.5 oz. lime juice
- 0.5 oz. cherry brandy
- 0.25 oz. Cointreau
- 0.25 oz. Benedictine
- A dash of Angostura bitters
- Club soda (to top up)
- Ice cubes
- Pineapple slice and maraschino cherry (for garnish)

## Directions:

1. Fill a cocktail shaker with ice cubes.

2. Add gin, pineapple juice, lime juice, cherry brandy, Cointreau, Benedictine, and Angostura bitters to the shaker.
3. Shake well for about 15 seconds to combine the ingredients.
4. Strain the mixture into a highball glass filled with ice cubes.
5. Top up with club soda.
6. Garnish with a pineapple slice and maraschino cherry.
7. Serve and enjoy!

**Nutrition:**
Calories: 170
Fat: 0g
Carbs: 15g
Protein: 0g

# Shirley Temple

**Preparation Time:** 5 minutes
**Cooking Time:** None
**Servings:** 1

### Ingredients:

- 1/2 cup lemon-lime soda
- 1/2 cup ginger ale
- 2 tablespoons grenadine syrup
- Maraschino cherry (for garnish)
- Ice cubes

### Directions:

1. Fill a glass with ice cubes.
2. Add lemon-lime soda and ginger ale into the glass.
3. Slowly pour in the grenadine syrup, allowing it to sink to the bottom.

4. Stir gently to combine the flavors.
5. Garnish with a maraschino cherry on top.
6. Serve immediately and enjoy!

**Nutrition:**
Calories: 90
Fat: 0g
Carbs: 22g
Protein: 0g

## Roy Rogers

**Preparation Time:** 5 minutes
**Cooking Time:** None
**Servings:** 1

### Ingredients:

- 1 oz. grenadine syrup
- 4 oz. cola
- Maraschino cherry (for garnish)
- Ice cubes

### Directions:

1. Fill a highball glass with ice cubes.
2. Pour grenadine syrup over the ice.
3. Slowly add cola to the glass, stirring gently to mix.
4. Garnish the drink with a maraschino cherry.
5. Serve immediately.

### Nutrition:
Calories: 85

Fat: 0g
Carbs: 22g
Protein: 0g

# Pink Lemonade

**Preparation Time:** 10 minutes
**Cooking Time:** None
**Servings:** 4

## Ingredients:

- 1 cup freshly squeezed lemon juice
- 1/2 cup granulated sugar
- 2 cups cranberry juice
- 3 cups cold water
- Ice cubes
- Lemon slices and mint sprigs for garnish

## Directions:

1. In a pitcher, combine the freshly squeezed lemon juice and granulated sugar. Stir until the sugar is dissolved.
2. Slowly pour in the cranberry juice and water, and mix well.
3. Add ice cubes to the pitcher and stir to chill the lemonade.
4. Once chilled, pour the pink lemonade into glasses filled with ice cubes.
5. Garnish with lemon slices and mint sprigs.

6. Serve immediately and enjoy!

**Nutrition:**
Calories: 90
Fat: 0g
Carbs: 24g
Protein: 0.5g

## Virgin Pina Colada

**Preparation Time:** 10 minutes
**Cooking Time:** None
**Servings:** 2

### Ingredients:

- 2 cups pineapple juice
- 1 cup coconut milk
- 1 cup crushed ice
- Pineapple wedge and maraschino cherry for garnish

### Directions:

1. In a blender, combine pineapple juice, coconut milk, and crushed ice.
2. Blend until smooth and frothy.
3. Pour into two glasses.
4. Garnish each glass with a pineapple wedge and a maraschino cherry.
5. Serve immediately and enjoy the tropical flavors!

### Nutrition:
Calories: 250

Fat: 14g
Carbs: 28g
Protein: 2g

# Fruit Punch

**Preparation Time:** 10 minutes
**Cooking Time:** None
**Servings:** 10-12

## Ingredients:

- 2 cups orange juice
- 2 cups pineapple juice
- 2 cups cranberry juice
- 1 cup lemon-lime soda
- 1 cup club soda
- 1/2 cup grenadine syrup
- 1 lemon, sliced
- 1 orange, sliced
- Ice cubes

## Directions:

1. In a large punch bowl, combine orange juice, pineapple juice, cranberry juice, lemon-lime soda, and club soda.
2. Stir in grenadine syrup for added sweetness and color.

3. Add lemon and orange slices to the punch bowl.
4. Add ice cubes to keep the punch chilled.
5. Stir the punch gently to mix all the flavors together.
6. Serve the fruit punch in glasses, making sure to include a few fruit slices in each glass.
7. Enjoy the refreshing taste of this classic fruit punch!

**Nutrition:** (per serving)
Calories: 120
Fat: 0g
Carbs: 30g
Protein: 0g

# Root Beer Float

**Preparation Time:** 5 minutes
**Cooking Time:** None
**Servings:** 1

## Ingredients:

- 2 scoops of vanilla ice cream
- 1 can or bottle of root beer

## Directions:

1. In a tall glass, carefully pour the root beer until it fills up about halfway.
2. Add the vanilla ice cream scoops on top of the root beer.
3. Slowly pour the remaining root beer over the ice cream to create a foamy head.
4. Allow the foam to settle for a moment before serving.
5. Serve immediately with a long spoon and a straw for sipping and scooping.

## Nutrition:
Calories: 335
Fat: 16g

Carbs: 43g
Protein: 5g

# Cherry Cola

**Preparation Time:** 10 minutes
**Cooking Time:** 5 minutes
**Servings:** 2

## Ingredients:

- 2 cups cola
- 1/4 cup cherry syrup
- 1 tablespoon fresh lemon juice
- 1/2 teaspoon vanilla extract
- Maraschino cherries, for garnish
- Ice cubes

## Directions:

1. In a pitcher, combine the cola, cherry syrup, lemon juice, and vanilla extract.
2. Stir well to combine all the ingredients.
3. Fill two glasses with ice cubes.
4. Pour the cherry cola mixture over the ice.
5. Garnish with a maraschino cherry on top of each glass.
6. Serve immediately and enjoy!

**Nutrition:**
Calories: 120
Fat: 0g
Carbs: 30g
Protein: 0g

# Orange Creamsicle Float

**Preparation Time:** 5 minutes
**Cooking Time:** None
**Servings:** 2

## Ingredients:

- 1 cup orange soda
- 1 cup vanilla ice cream
- Whipped cream (optional)
- Orange zest for garnish (optional)

## Directions:

1. In a tall glass, add half a cup of orange soda.
2. Drop two scoops of vanilla ice cream into the glass.
3. Pour the remaining orange soda slowly over the ice cream.
4. Gently stir with a spoon to mix the flavors.
5. Top with whipped cream and orange zest, if desired.
6. Serve immediately with a straw and a long spoon.

**Nutrition:**
Calories: 230
Fat: 7g
Carbs: 39g
Protein: 3g

## **Chocolate Egg Cream**

**Preparation Time:** 5 minutes
**Cooking Time:** None
**Servings:** 1

### Ingredients:

- 2 tablespoons chocolate syrup
- 1/2 cup sparkling water
- 1/4 cup whole milk
- 2 tablespoons seltzer water
- A few drops of vanilla extract

### Directions:

1. In a tall glass, pour in the chocolate syrup.
2. Slowly pour the whole milk over the syrup while stirring gently.
3. Add the sparkling water and stir until well combined.
4. Pour in the seltzer water and stir gently once again.
5. Finish by adding a few drops of vanilla extract for additional flavor.
6. Your Chocolate Egg Cream is now ready to be enjoyed!

**Nutrition:**
Calories: 180
Fat: 3g
Carbs: 35g
Protein: 7g

## Sparkling Raspberry Limeade

**Preparation Time:** 10 minutes
**Cooking Time:** None
**Servings:** 4

### Ingredients:

- 1 cup fresh raspberries
- 1/2 cup fresh lime juice
- 1/2 cup granulated sugar
- 2 cups sparkling water
- Ice cubes

### Directions:

1. In a blender or food processor, blend the fresh raspberries until smooth.
2. Strain the raspberry puree through a fine-mesh sieve into a pitcher to remove any seeds.
3. Add the fresh lime juice and granulated sugar to the pitcher and stir until the sugar is dissolved.
4. Fill the pitcher with ice cubes and stir to chill the mixture.

5. Slowly pour in the sparkling water and gently stir to combine.
6. Serve the Sparkling Raspberry Limeade over ice and garnish with additional fresh raspberries or lime slices if desired.

**Nutrition:**
Calories: 100
Fat: 0g
Carbs: 26g
Protein: 0g

Printed in Dunstable, United Kingdom